PSYCHOLOGY BEHIND QUITTING

UNDERSTANDING TRUE REASONS

MALLIKARJUNA SASALWAD
MUDDUGALMATH

ISBN 979-888629109-4

This book is dedicated to my grandfather & grandmother

Contents

Preface

They were at top positions of corporate ladder with highest level of respect, bulky remunerations and hefty facilities, still these top leaders are stepping away!! They were reassessing their role in work-life balance situation. Some were not happy, some are burned out, and some want to achieve something else.

Psychology behind Quitting is eye opener book which tells the truths of what is running in CEO's burning mind, reveals true secrets behind quitting of top executives, how it feels to be when you reach that position, how long you can hold off that position? And finally what is beyond it !!!

Inspired by "**Great Resignation**" movement in United States of America post global pandemic, this book book on has been written on true experiences on how life of top executives, as well as normal workers life has been changed drastically. Unveils secrets of what a true human being need!!!

Author name: Mallikarjuna Sasalwad Muddugalmath
Date: 28-Feb-2022

Acknowledgements

Thanks to my family, friends and colleagues who helped in my Author journey. Special thanks to David Gelles, Newyork time through which I inspired to write this book.

Prologue

It has been more than 2 years since the on set of the global pandemic, world has become almost stand still!! The global pandemic has changed the whole where it was heading, life of people has been changed drastically. Millions of people have lost lives of near and dean ones.

Some have lost their jobs, some have lost their business, some class of people were over working and other class was job less.

Tsunami of Covid has left fear, anxiety for most, it has given the courage to stand up for some others. Each and every phase of life should be taken with positive attitude in sailing the life boat until it reaches end.

While the situation has thought that any time, anything can change. Nothing is permanent in life. Driving factors of life like food, shelter, job, and security will continue to get us moving. However, as you reach the top positions or near top positions, gives you realization that you are actually not looking for that "thing" in there.

Out of short within 2 years, life has taught us that life is not all about money, job, top positions but something beyond.

Something beyond not necessarily mean, materialistic aspect of life but more on experiences side of life. What is the point of getting "Rolls Royce" when you are aged enough that you can't drive? What is the point, if your family miss you on an important family occasion or function? You are busy in meeting client presentation. What is the use of vacation days your company offering, when kids needed most of your time and you cannot give it.

This book gives real world examples of Psychology behind human mind. The urgency, curiosity and need to go to "Top", then try to reach "bottom". This roller coaster ride is not about money or position but more of human sentiments, family connects, bondage we have with friends we have built us around!!

Back to Basics

"The only way you can stay on top is to remember to touch bottom and get back to basics"
-Share Black

As technology tends to drive us faster and faster, faster, but we as human beings need to understand that our body, mind and soul are not made up of machines nor technology. It is still the basics which are driving us. These are still the fundamentals that taking us ahead.

We need a healthy body to work, healthy mind and food food for nutrition and good thoughts emotions for keeping us motivated. Good money for meeting the daily needs and good time for boosting our emotions.

Success is not measured by sitting in corner office nor how much money you made in your life time. Success is measured by how many people you have helped to come up in life. How many kids you have made them enable to get education who were deprived of education? How many elderly people you have helped crossing the zebra crossing or living in poor old age homes.

At each stage of life, we should take a pause, look at mirror, asses where we are, what we want, why we want and which way I want to go. If you answer these simple questions, then self-realization and self-awareness will happen internally. Then I don't think you have to tumble when you go up there!! You know what I meant!!

Build your base, your families and next generation foundations stronger not by technology but by trusting values and emotions.

Kindly pour in the amount of time required for each of these when needed. Spend quality time with your friends, kids and relatives.

Reunion on old friends in simple walk or party, which gets you feeling of connect both physical and emotional. Rejuvenate, be happy!! Please don't overwork. if you can't do, just be true to yourselves and say you cannot do it. If something happens to you, your family is the one who will cry for you not corporate world nor your boss!!

I am not saying you should not work, please don't mistaken me. When you are doing work, do work, when you are having fun, have fun. Don't mix up!!

Time for yourself

"Do not let a day go by without taking some time for yourself".

As you may have seen in the recent trend in United States of America, "Great Resignations", approximately 4.5 million people left their jobs only in November. This number exceeds the number than any other month before.

This trend of greater resignations not only confined to only the class of workers in IT sector or Medical field but across many other sectors. Many of executives leaving top jobs are never have to worry about paying bills or managing their finances.

One of primer force driving these resignations is not getting enough time for yourself or your family. As you move up the ladder, the more responsibilities you need to manage, you need to interact with more people, more meetings!! More pressure!! More deliverables!!

Unless you are very solid on your fundamentals on your body, emotions, energy, at some point in time, you are doing to be state of "Burn Out". This burn out is not because of single reason but over a period of time, you stop focussing your inner wellbeing, not draining out your useless thoughts before sleep, keeping lot of worries about work, anxiety about your upcoming project deadline.

Slowly steadily these will accumulated in your mind, will become thoughts, unless there is a cleansing mechanism, your mind will become like balloon of thoughts. More you feed, more it takes, bulkier it will become. Some point time, boom! it will burst out !!

To avoid burn outs, individual's first workout on oneself. Give yourself the much needed break or time. Time is biggest healer in the world. No matter how big is your worry, it has the potential to solve given a sufficient amount of time.

If you make a habit of spending time within your own body, mind and soul, the rest of material aspects of life can be dealt easily.

One of best method to spend time with your self is by doing Meditation early in morning when there are no disturbances and also in night before sleep. Disconnect from gadgets at-least 2 hours before sleep and focus only on your breath closing your eyes. Praising the god for what all he has given us and starting day with positive thoughts will boost our energy levels throughout the day.

CHAPTER THREE

Vitamin - M

"Money doesn't grow on trees"

We are all in the rat race, race towards money, position, job and what not!! But out of all Money is the most important driving factor. To accompany our basic needs of day definitely power of money is needed, no doubt about it.

Unless you are born in a rich family or gifted rich, most of people fall into working category. In a research made in 2021, employment to population ratio worldwide was estimated to be approximately 55.9% indicating that just over half of global working age population were employed. How about the rest of the crowd? They are either kids, older generation or people who cannot work. So in general, each and every person has one additional responsibility as a whole!

From my point of view, in today's generation has access to most of basic needs like food, shelter, etc. even though it may be accurate across the globe, but due to excessive help from government to below poverty line people, most of these necessities have been taken care.

But the human mind is not designed to settle at any lower levels, unless you have self-made boundary or satisfaction or great Himalayan yogi who has attained that great sense of satisfaction.

Once the basic needs of finance are met, the next is good to have, luxury and many more. There is no limit to monkey mind. These will go on and on and so on ......

The other way to escape the money mind what I have realized is through feeling of contentment. Let me give a very simple example though our Indian traditions.

In any sacred functions like Pooja, marriage or ceremony of elders usually the tradition is to feed the hungry for guests and who are in need until they are full. At least to large number of people to best of that person can support. The more you serve, the more people eat, the greeted is satisfaction. Good Karma the man gets. Feeding the people considered one of sacred acts of humans in many cultures as well. Only when man is full stomach, if you server more, he will say "Enough of it", I am done, this is feeling of contentment.

However, if you give bag full of money to the people who have come to attend your ceremony, still the contentment will not come. Greedy mind will ask for more & more!!!

CHAPTER FOUR

Social Status

"To be truly positive in the eyes of some, you have to risk appearing negative in the eyes of others"

In the new world of digitals, Facebook, what's app, Instagram, twitter the eagerness to share the doing's, happening's, your stories has become more pre-dominant than ever in younger generation. I see lot of people sometime including myself, getting stressed if we can't see our movie gadgets for more than an hour or so.

Notion of social status is another driver factor which will take you nowhere. A good and healthy comparison is always helps. In fact lot of cultures, corporates have the habit of comparison among the peer group in terms of how they are doing.

Socioeconomic status is the social standing or class of individual group examinations. Socioeconomic status often revel in-equalities in access to resources, also issues related to privilege, power and control.

The fear of keeping the social or economic or both as an individual person creates lot of stress. Sometimes it creates the positive growth also, however it may not be the case always. Trying to become, something you are not, is not what you want.

Trying to show something, which is unreal, show offs , sets unrealistic expectations to viewers If you take a photo with a car standing in parking lot, which is let us say "Rolls Royce", the first impression of viewer, this sets the wrong expectations. In turn yield wrong results. This if true not only in profession relationship but rather in any kind of relationship no matter you deal with.

Piece of friendly advice below would help one to escape from phobia of maintaining the social status.

Do's:

- Be honest, be yourself always
- Don't over exaggerate things
- Be true and don't compare yourself with anyone else
- Every individual has positive and negative aspects.
- Separate private, business, and profession related posts in any social media sites.
- Seek feedback if needed

Dont's:

- Don't over react on social media
- Don't be jealous of someone status.
- Don't give negative feedback
- Don't use foul language

CHAPTER FIVE

Stress Factor

"More smiling, less worrying"

For 20 years, Rebecca Hellman had a way up the career ladder in health care industry. In 2019, she left a senior marketing position at cardinal health, a major pharmaceutical distributor to become chief marketing officer of Oliver startup based on Columbus, Ohio. That work with hospitals "I thought that was task leap and would make" she said.

But as the pandemic work on, Ms. Hellman found herself close than expected to front line of fight against Covid-19. All day, she would hear stories about over taxed emergency rooms and rising deaths counts.

At the same time, Ms. Hellman, a single mother of four was trying to keep her children on task during remote learning while maintaining her composure on ceaseless zoom meetings.

"It was stressful" she said, "I had a moment where I was like "Is this what is is supposed to be like?"

That simple question was the first crack in a broader questioning of her Identify and purpose.

MS Hellmann had resolved to make drastic change in August, 2020 she quit.

She mentions "I had no idea what I was doing, but I know this wasn't it" she said.

Over the past year, Mr. Hellman has turned to mindfulness meditation, first as a way to find peace and now potentially as a new career. She went on weeklong meditation, kayak trip in Mexico, completed yearlong mindfulness training course and now begin her own mindfulness coaching business.

She believes, she is doing what she needs to be doing, far from corporate, I will either come back and do that , or we will see where this leads to me " she said. "You only have one life"

The life of us no different than any one of us, isn't it? In a highly competitive, digital fast moving world all things need rigor, fastness. This will create at every layer of work force "stress". But as long as you love what you do, it may not cause real damage. But, if you are not, then life becomes the life of MS. Hellmann one day you will feel the "burnout"

CHAPTER SIX

Under the good leader

"If your actions inspire others to dream more, learn more, do more and become more, you are a leader"

No matter what you do in life, if you are not under a good leader or rather I call "Guru" in any field, you will not be able to achieve what you wanted to achieve. Each step you headed needs someone who know, trusts us and gives direction of correct path to grow, achieve desired outcomes.

According to research study by Rose Torres who has taught and mentored hundreds of top CEO and CFO conducted a research on what are traits of good leader in 21st century. There are numerous books if you google it out, but we are looking for something latest and based out of research.

The research study reveals that there are 3 most common traits or behaviors all sacksful leaders are tend to made of.

1. Where are you looking to anticipate change
2. What is the diversity of your network measure?
3. Are you courageous enough to abandon past?

If you look at great leaders like Gandhi, Nelson Mandela who fought for freedom. Their rational way was completely opposite direction of crowd. When world was getting violent and speaking of war, they thought peace, love, patiently gave success over a period of time.

It definitely takes some amount of luck and if you are under a good leader but also learning the qualities of leader.

Leader should have vision, anticipate the change in business, technology, methodology is no matter piece of cake. One of best example would like to give is, in 1970 champaklal Choksey, the dominant visionary founder of Asian paints, spend 8 crore buying the India's 1st super computer decades before ISRO, IIT or any other Indian conglomerate. World finest ERP implementation is done at Asian Paints.

Diversity of network and discontinuing to abandon comfort zone, diving into new areas with calculated risks are other 2 qualities you should be looking for your leader.

Let me give an example, one of slipper making company called "Relaxo" small vendor in skipper making business. During those times all leading manufacturer like Nike, Adidas used to outsource these making process to external vendors. But management team of Relaxo decided to take exact opposite direction. Instead of outsourcing, they reinvested profits for building manufacturing plants. Because of which they were able to build a dominant market for the products they produce and give extra margin. No other competitor can give lesser the price of Relaxo products as they have their own plants and margins.

CHAPTER SEVEN

Self-Motivation

"No one can motive you until you motivate yourself"
No matter what external forces are towards your job, business or any other thing you are doing, unless you a self-motivated person or soul, you will not be able to find peace or contentment anywhere.

If you look at baby playing all by itself, it can play with a still for 3-4 hours. For it to playful, it don't need any forces or high fi gadgets. Whatever it gets on the ground, he can play for hours. So what is the keeps motivated individuals??

According to research study by Scott Gilles there are 4 basic things in general for any individual to be self-motivated.

1. **Perception of Competence**
2. **Consequences drive us**
3. **Perceive choice**
4. **Community.**

Perception of competence if if a person is capable to doing something technical, managerial or any business , a piece of work or building a master piece, he should have confidence of doing it and necessary competence .

Consequence drive us: If you know that you are doing something very important and worthwhile then you will with utmost due diligence. Tiny changes of good thinking will give enormous results over a period of time. Similarly, if you are good leader, you will need to ensure the importance of work others are doing. Once the importance is set, I am sure no person will not neglect unless if there is a genuine reason.

Perceive choice: If a person is given choices rather than no choice or single choice, the chances are better off doing. Not because, there were more, simple reason of choice is being made by same person. Try all in your daily activities. I am sure you will get results.

Community: Humans are more of social animals. We have feelings, emotions, love, affection and other sentiments associated. As we move up in our personal and professional life, the more it important of being identified as social wellbeing. Your good work being recognized in your connections, network will very much make stand out of your way.

No matter what you do in life, if you are not under a good leader or rather I call "Guru" in any field, you will not be able to achieve what you wanted to achieve. Each step you headed needs someone who know, trusts us and gives direction of correct path to grow, achieve desired outcomes.

CHAPTER EIGHT

Change Is the only Constant

"True life is lived when tiny changes occur"
Change of technology moving at very faster pace than ever. It has not only become difficult for a common man who eventually become the users of these technologies or software's, apps. If you look at the other side of story, for software companies, these new things need to be adapted as soon as possible. If not, they will sooner or later become non-competent and will be left behind.

This is not only on the technical staff and end users, to manage operate, leaders in the industry will need a new skills outlined in previous chapter. The need for change gives opportunities to grow, at the same time creates lot of pressure behind.

As a matter of fact, if you look at example of frog, when put into vessel containing water. When water is heated initially, the frog will try to adjust the body temperature to outside warm water.

When the temperature is increased the frog will continue to adjust, adjust, at last when it cannot tolerate the heat, it tries to jump. But, now it cannot, simple reason, it has spent all of energy in trying to adjust but it was unable to make right decision.

I am quite sure by this time, you would have got glimpse of what I am trying to say. Change is necessary but if it is "burnout" then you should put a full stop.

Reason top executives change more often than needed, the amount of heat they can't withstand or not be able to tolerate.

End of day if you are not happy or your family is not happy, you are unable to spend quality time with yourself or family, kids, relatives then there is no meaning to it. Constantly self asses, self-commit and get outside feedback based on which make a move.

No matter what external forces are towards your job, business or any other thing you are doing, unless you a self-motivated person or soul, you will not be able to find peace or contentment anywhere.

CHAPTER NINE

Opportunities & Rewards

"Opportunities don't happen you create them"
Pandemic has taught us that these increased demand for remote workers, digitalization in all aspects of world created lot of work across industry. This drift has caused the movement in revolutionary way in IT product and service industry.

Millions of job opportunities were created due to huge demand across the globe. Attrition rates has been in double digits. Human resources have been fighting to retain key employees all over. Salaries outside have doubled, tripled for talented pool of technologists. Extra remuneration packages, perks to attract young to mid-level talent has been done at large scale.

If you are doing same amount of work with better salary, who does not want it. Best to utilize the cycle to get favor out of it. Remuneration packages would vary from skill to skill and run different across.

Anand who was developer and wanted to go earn more & wanted to visit onsite unable to get a chance in current company. He could get both within a very span of time with double digit hike. He quit.

No matter what other factors, but rewards and packages will definitely one of most proven ways behind a quitting individual.

Similary, employers on the other hand facing lot of challenges due to the fact of lot of mid and junior level employees switchin jobs within a very short period of time. Human resources are struggling to fill the vacancies the companies have.

CHAPTER TEN

Politics

"An empty stomach is not good political adviser"

In the corporate world, more you grow up the ladder, the bigger are the challenges you face or most of you face related to office politics. This is not only true at all level, but becomes more evident at top levels of the ladder.

Politics based on the caste, gender, religion and any other factors should be completely removed in any organization. However, since this is more of people driven approach, more tools to enable the data process based on the real facts and work done needs to enabled to avoid any of employees leaving due to office politics.

According to DDI research 57% of employees quit because of their boss. But why? 14% left multiple companies, 43% left only one company, 32% thought about leaving, 12% never thought about leaving.

Basically there are 4 major issues with this:

1. **People quit bosses**
2. **Office politics**
3. **Managers are drowning in touch conversations**

4. Sense of performance.

The research proves people leave managers not companies. If managers are not enabled to handle right amount of people with right attitude, losers would be companies.

Managers and individual contributors alike two chief **sources of stress.** Not enough time to do everything and dealing with politics. Senior leaders also recognize how busy frontline leaders are cling to many responsibilities and lack of time as top barrier for success.

Managers drowning in tough conversation: senior leaders point out top weakness of frontline managers is their ability to have difficult conversation with reportees.

Move to leadership is typically – Unexpected: 70% of frontline managers weren't expecting the promotion to leadership where as 20% of were executed by prospect of leadership. 17 % only took role because seemed like good step.

Pandemic has taught us that these increased demand for remote workers, digitalization in all aspects of world created lot of work across industry. This drift has caused the movement in revolutionary way in IT product and service industry.

CHAPTER ELEVEN

Environment

"The environment makes our character"

As a manager and member of recruiting staff, I also take lot of interviews. Usually in the interviews lasts about a 1 hour to 1.5 hours per candidate. In this very short span of time, team needs to assess the candidate is right fit for role and company.

To assess the personal traits and behavioral aspects, usually common questions being asked are:

Why are you changing company? What are challenges faced? What is the expectation from you in current company? What if expectations are not met?

Lot of candidates previously switch lasted for 6 months an year in Industry. Most common answer about these are **"Environment"** of company. Candidate's area of interest do not match their current working conditions. So, over a very short period of time, employees gets demotivated and starts to look for another.

Growth oriented, conducive and positive environment is essential part of any job. Every day we need to spend at-least 8-9 hours of working. So if you or any person dint find it challenging or not getting curios about the work due to same old mundane type of work, no new learnings, lack of opportunities in required skills cause lot of damage to companies leaving behind talented pool of resources.

Even though there is no single stop solution for this problem, employees and employers continue to strive towards getting right workplace for employees.

CHAPTER TWELVE

Family

"A family in harmony will proper in everything"
Mr. Rahul was in line for big job as chief operating officer of VMWare the large cloud computing firm, he was a top contender to replace the departing chief executive.

But in the end, the CEO role went to someone else last year. Mr. Rahul left the company. "It was good time for me1" he said. "I 'have never really taken a break in life"

Now, he finds himself as abundance of time to spend with this loved ones. He has got his faith back at him home. His 4 children are high school and he is soaking up as much time with them as he can. He say "I love to drive for them in dropping to school and games"

The pandemic has opened eyes to lot many that he did, he said "I want to make blessing to everyone I come in touch"

So another key driving factor if you are unable to spend quality time with your loved ones, sooner or later, heat will blow up some or other day.

Keeping a balance between work and family life is like two parallel tracks of train. The more it runs parallel the better it is. If you get overloaded with too much work not give time for family then family life will going to take hit but on flip side if you focus only on the family, the finances going to take a toll unless you have built a very strong income streams.

CHAPTER THIRTEEN

Right Job

"Finding the right work is like discovering your own soul in the world"

The notion of "**Right job**" is very abstract and these should not be single definition as this is logical to each person's perception. What is right for me, may not be right for anyone else.

As long long as you love your job or what you are doing as work and business, if it gets you sense of fulfillment, you should be OK. Running behind good remuneration, new technology, new company, and new country and so on will continue. But if you are not happy inside or if you are not enjoying the position, your definition of Right job will not holds good. Because if you are not happy, you want put focus, if you won't focus, you won't give 100%.

As chief Marketing officer for one of reputed company, the industrial conglomerate, Mr. Raman at the age of 50, has reached top. He was drawing a handsome salary, living comfortable life in New Jersey. Leading branding for biggest manufacturer in world.

But, last year he had reached a unfamiliar and somewhat confusion in his mind "I started not to be happy"

For many years, he would run out to go excited about work. But, while Mr. Raman had fulfilling life when it came to office, thrill was gone one day he "Quit"

Now, in the free time he says "The day I left, I committed to taking on something that I love to do but never had time to do, which was writing" he said. In addition, he is giving precious time to his teenagers.

CHAPTER FOURTEEN

Managing body & Monkey Mind

"Try to have monkey skill, not monkey mind"

As one of neuro scientist explains in one of her great talks "How our thoughts and emotions control our bodies and opposite can be done with little of her small research with group of people" which is controlling our emotions through our body.

When we are stressed out, in anxiety, anger look at the way we breach. Our breath become shallow, rapid and fast so what we do? We put cross fingers, taking knuckles out, squeezing our neck or putting hands on your forehead.

By these behavioral body aspects someone can easily realize you are stressed out. If you continue to work or continue in high stressed environment definitely the body will sooner or later take the burden.

There are tiny tweaks which can be adapted to bring lot of change which eventually bring change in your thoughts and emotions. Instead of feeling fickleness, your thoughts will become stable.

Important, small tips in this chapter will help you manager your mind & emotions better:

1. Focus on breath always. Correct your body postures while sitting, standing and talking
2. Ensure you are in right spirit ahead of any tough schedule.
3. Correct your body postures, sit straight, chest wide open and arms free.
4. Ensure you practice, practice, practice which makes perfection
5. Medidate when you go before sleep and when u wake up.
6. Limit usage of gadgets before sleep.
7. Plan ahead of day's schedule as much as possible.
8. Thanks and appreciate god in every aspects of life has given to you.
9. Start with a smile always even if you cannot.
10. Don't react.
11. If something stressful comes, take time to respond.
12. When in anger, take longer deeper breathe at-least 10. The more you do, better it is.

Go for a simply walk, chat with family, do yoga or medication in morning and evening, laugh out loud when needed. Talk to friends more often, go to relatives and frieds marriage functions. These are small opputunies which brings us together and make us rejuvenrate ourselves. Nothing is permanent in this world, but time you spend for yourself, for your family, near and dear ones will definitely give you back in some way or other.

CHAPTER FIFTEEN

Summary

If you are reading until here means, I am sure you would have known reasons behind why people quit. As I mentioned, human beings are more emotional, social creatures than materilistic. They need freedom, they need happiness, they need social status, they need motivation. Simply running behind a top position, if you are not capable of only brings you down, no sooner than later. In this era of digitization, even a machine can do any type of work but what is needed is true connect, empathy and happiness that we do & interact with everyday life to grow and sustain. I hope you find enyoing this short book.